Ordinary Magic

Other Books by Alison Stone

Dangerous Enough (Presa Press, 2014)
Borrowed Logic (Dancing Girl Press, 2014)
From the Fool to the World (Parallel Press, 2011)
They Sing at Midnight (Many Mountains Moving Press, 2003)

Ordinary Magic

Alison Stone

NYQ Books™

The New York Quarterly Foundation, Inc.
New York, New York

NYQ Books™ is an imprint of The New York Quarterly Foundation, Inc.

The New York Quarterly Foundation, Inc.
P. O. Box 2015
Old Chelsea Station
New York, NY 10113

www.nyq.org

First Edition

Set in New Baskerville

Layout by Raymond P. Hammond

Cover Design by Raymond P. Hammond

Original Tarot Card Art by Alison Stone | www.stonetarot.com

Author Photo by Michael Stone

Library of Congress Control Number: 2016941107

ISBN: 978-1-63045-031-1

Ordinary Magic

Thank You

Thanks to Dzvinia Orlowsky, Kathi Aguero, and Thom Ward for suggestions on earlier versions of these poems. Thanks to Bill Packard, for support way back when, and to Michael, for support now.

While many sources have contributed to my understanding of the tarot, I am most indebted to Rachel Pollack, whose *Seventy-Eight Degrees of Wisdom* books were essential.

Acknowledgments

Poems in this book, some in earlier versions, have or will appear in the following:

Art Times: Death

Artful Dodge: Rats Live On No Evil Star

Barrow Street: Temperance

Big Scream: As Though You Owned that Time, My Brother's Collections, Memorial Park

Center: The Wheel of Fortune, The World

Event: Sweets

First Literary Review - East: The Fool, The High Priestess, The Emperor

First of the Month: The Lovers, Justice, Judgment, The Tower, Mother Lion, Steve Jobs, Fa La La, Love Song to Lou Reed

Forge: As Though You Owned that Time, First Pomegranate, Blues Café, Friendly Floatees, Slowly, Dangerous, Tether, Rope, The Story, Euridyce to Orpheus

Iconoclast: Why, Because, Hep C, Forty-Seven

Lilith: Lilith to Adam (titled Lilith Speaks)

Many Mountains Moving: The Sun, Viviene Eliot

The Mom Egg: Festival of Light

New York Quarterly: The Workshop Leader tells us to Become a Power Animal (titled Animal Games), Lilith's Daughter on a Date, Better than Sex

One: Prometheus Examines his Motives

Perceptions: Galatea to Pygmalion

Poetry: Brandeis Senior Year

Poetry International: Divorce Court

San Pedro River Review: Unemployed

Slipstream: Hercules in Retirement

Star*Line: The Emperor

Solstice: Persephone After, Boy on a Hot House

Fa La La also appeared in the anthology *Brigit: Sun of Womanhood*. The Lovers also appeared in *First of the Year, volume II.* Justice also appeared in *First of the Year, volume III.* Mother Lion also appeared in *First of the Year, volume IV.* Steve Jobs and "Adam and Eve, Not Adam and Steve" appeared in *First of the Year, volume V.* A Bird! A Plane! A Frog! appeared in *Drawn to Marvel: Poems from the Comic Books.* My Brother's Collections appeared in *Siblings: Our First Macrocosm.* The Emperor, The Lovers, and Temperance appeared in *Arcana: A Tarot Anthology.*

The poems in the Major Arcana were published as a chapbook, *From the Fool to the World,* by Parallel Press.

Better than Sex was awarded the Madeline Sadin Award by the *New York Quarterly.*

Contents

The Major Arcana

The Minor Arcana

Pentacles

In memory of my mother,
Deanne Cohn Stone

The Major Arcana

0. The Fool

Say *yes*. Don't look.
Leap!

Every journey starts
with the eager dog of the heart.

Zero is an egg
that holds all numbers.

If you won't dance,
then who's the fool?

Inside my cloth bag—apple,
table, stallion, sky.

Come! The rich
cliff tempts like wine.

I. The Magician

No rabbit up my sleeve, no hidden door.
As above, so below—the sun's
red laughter, the roses'
soft red mouths.

Sure I juggle planets, twist
balloons into a zoo; but the real
work is to hold two wands—
one raised, the other
pointed to the ground—
to let power flow through you like song.

Trying to hoard God, lovers
swoon and seekers speak
in tongues. Mere party tricks!
Common as a deck of marked cards. Any amateur
can saw a box in half, his blond assistant
safely scrunched to one side,
can draw applause
escaping from fake locks.

The true magician
summons heaven down to earth,
where it can blossom.

II. The High Priestess

Red of pomegranate, red of blood.
Hollow men, does my blood
scare you? And you, timid ladies
who won't claim my name?

There are lands you enter
after midnight, pages you
can't read with open eyes.

Cut like a foreskin from history,
I know the mind
is just a small thing, tight
as the throat of the child whose father gloats,
Eve from Adam's rib! waving
the Bible in triumph.
She is wan and bookless. Her bones
are not her own.

III. The Empress

Languid sun
honeys my skin;
toes scrunch
lush grass. Fingering
the pearls and planets draped
around my neck, I recline
near the river
and watch babies suckle,
children tumble in the grain.
While lovers lope
beneath branches that sag
from the weight of dark fruit,
birds shove beaks
into the sweetness.

You are all my children.
Your body knows
to trust rough bark, to listen
to ears of corn.
Do not lament
to the sky, seeking
distant heaven. This world
you drag your feet upon
is paradise.

IV. The Emperor

Every life needs edges.
I protect you from the meadow's
wanton splendor,
passion running amok.

Lean against my law
the way a child lets go
into a father's arms. Pruned
and tethered vines bear stronger fruit.

Defy me
if the sobbing
of jailed innocents
grows louder than rain.

Kill me
when the names
for animals and sky
replace the animals and sky.

V. The High Priest

My flock,
talking to God is effortless.
<u>Please</u> and <u>help</u>
fall from our lips
as easily as loose rock
drops from the face of a cliff.
Listening is harder work.
Garbled to the novice, God's voice
needs translation. Without a teacher,
His verbs won't unlock.

Used to be
they learned Latin,
used to be they kept
their doubts to themselves. Now
even the faithful study Darwin,
even the devoted ask
where the collection money
goes. My own doubt
turns to pebbles in my mouth.
I confess—I envy monks
who set themselves on fire.
Such spectacular prayer!
In dreams, humble sparrows fly
with eagle wings. Every mumbling
servant longs to sing.

VI. The Lovers

Coiled around this tree for centuries, I've seen
the Bible's myth of sin and fig leaves twist

an older tale of sacred fruit whose juice
unlocks the door to paradise.

Truth is, a man lives in his parents' dreams
until lust lets him go; an angel

only hovers when a woman
holy with desire grabs her lover's hand.

Don't believe the story of a cherub with a crossbow
binding fools in blind devotion.

Love is always a choice.

VII. The Chariot

I win! I have harnessed
fear and passion,
antique beasts
whose riddles can't kill me.

Now waves are dragged
by the full moon of my heart.
The stars spell out my name.

My one eye misses nothing.
I am a language without adjectives, a diamond
in the setting of itself.

I want wolves to lick my feet. I want
swine to turn to princes when I speak.
I want my sweat to smell like nectar.
I want doubt to melt in my mouth.

Other beings are tied with string,
jerked by the breeze
that is my breath. I am the spider
in the center of the web.

When I cough, mountains fall.
When I am angry, the old die in their beds.
If I tear a fingernail, a child
is born without limbs.

(The tethered sphinxes
paw the ground and stare.)

I can look nowhere
without seeing myself. My giant
jaws chew up the world
until there is no world.

VIII. Strength

The unheard heart
grows fangs and fur.
Fat with need,
this rough beast
roars behind heavy bars.
Will you stay
when I unlock the gate?

Teach me
your secrets, animal—
the dreams you ate.
Release the worried bones.

Armed with flowers,
I guide the jaws.

IX. The Hermit

Beard to indicate sagacity,
a firm yet gentle voice—I know
what you're expecting when you call, know you need
permission masked as a command:
Turn from money, love. Ignore
the mortgage. Leave your name.
My costumes change through the ages.
Right now hooded cloaks
are popular, as well as the spectacles
and notepad of a kindly analyst.
The journey is always the same,
and I've guided it so many times, I fantasize
about retiring. Days in the garden,
nights by the fire, small questions only: Coffee
or chamomile? Crossword or book?
But *when the student is ready,* etc.
so here we go. Follow me
into this grove of silver trees
where wild cries cut the dark and memories
hang like bats. The spooked heart
crying, *Turn back now,* the soul
a small white moth drawn by my lantern's beam.

X. The Wheel of Fortune

From my eternal turning, everything
that falls can rise and what goes up
can plummet like a torn balloon.
I am painted with the law of fate.

What falls can rise and what goes up…
An old story, thick with questions.
I am painted with the law.
The breath of this law is concealed in its letters.

History thickens with questions.
The way the moon masks herself as a woman
and the breath of the law is concealed in its letters,
the Grail hides in your kitchen sink.

Old moon masked as a woman,
soul obscured by flesh,
the Grail hides in your kitchen sink.
Wealth passes into winter, war into song.

The soul costumed as flesh
can plummet like a torn balloon.
Wealth passes into winter, war into song.
From my eternal turning, everything.

XI. Justice

I am not blind,
you are blind—

wandering memory's forest, scratched
by branches, cursing the dark

while birds cry in the poplars
and the damp earth reeks. A thick snake

slithers and coils.
Which scares you more,

to believe that life is unfair
or to believe that life is fair?

XII. The Hanged Man

Eyes level with lilies, feet in the clouds—
Every day I dangle, habits
and ambitions fly away
like dust motes from a beaten rug.

Nothing sways me,
not the gray-eyed lady
or the neighbors' gossip, not the stack of mail.
Yes, I'm thirsty, cold, I ache

from so much blood to the brain, also the perching
and pecking of curious birds;
but I hang
tranquil as the lake beneath my hair.

Join me on this tree, head under heels.
Surrender
will transform the rope around your leg
into a lover's hand.

XIII. Death

What will it take to reassure you?
I don't bring oblivion. The old self
needs to be sloughed off like skin.
Think of me as cosmetologist, not fiend.

Why suck the dry breast
of the past?
The mask is not the face.
Even breath is not the soul,
although the body has
no other wings.

Deep Moss shadowing the lids, cheeks
flushed with Pink Impermanence…

You know me when you clean
hairs from your comb,
when you lie down with your lover,
bone to bone.

XIV. Temperance

Of course moderation is a piece of cake
for me; I am an angel.
I have had eternity to master balance,
and besides, it's easy to stay
calm in any storm
when a rainbow arcs perpetually
above my head like a giant umbrella.
I understand you are only human.
Still, why let yourself be bumped from center
by recycled heart hungers or the lust beast.
Throw away your book of rules. Stop boring everyone
with resolutions. Just plant
one foot on land, the other
in the cold school of the sea.

XV. The Devil

There is no heaven, nothing more than this
dull job, poor health, lifeless relationship.
Dance to the music of the fire's hiss.

Leave any time you like—the loose
chains I drape don't bind you. Have a nice trip.
There is no heaven, nothing more than this.

Life burns. Sex is the only balm. Don't miss
any chance to screw, lie, rest, repeat. Clap
your bodies to the music. Fires hiss:

The soul's a pretty fiction. Take the kiss
of your familiar anguish, its warm lap.
There is no heaven, nothing more than this.

Since this base world is all there is, practice
gulping money and awards. Never stop
dancing. Greed's music is the fire's hiss.

I offer you respite from the abyss
of futile wishes. Hope is the real trap.
There is no heaven, nothing more than this.
Dance to the music of the fire's hiss.

XVI. The Tower

Stones of money,
bricks of sex divide you

from the wind, the wild stars.
Trapped inside my walls, you

miss the tocsins.
Pressure's building fast.

Do you think
lightning comes from outside?

Too late now. The bolt
sears me like love.

I'm crumbling.

Which god
will you pray to

as you leap
into a sky alive with fire?

XVII. The Star

Hush.
Lie down by the still pool,
the sharp hills blurred to shadow.

Why do you think
I'm featured in so many lullabies?

If light were music,
mine would be the tune
your mother crooned as you,
the day's bumps and abandonments
erased, sank milk-drunk into sleep.

XVIII. The Moon

The lines of your features blur in my light.
Oceans foam. Waves reach to gather my light.

Always voluptuous, I sometimes hide
all but one small sliver of my light.

Don't say I reflect the sun; I transform
his garish rays to silver. My light

turns to jewels bared teeth of dog and wolf, their howls
mingling. Shadows devour the polite

garden. Souls of the mad float up to seek me.
Frenzied, they circle forever in flight.

The swing roped to the oak tree sways; a red
ball drops near Mother, young, her hair of light.

From the lake's belly, a giant crayfish
rises, crawls from water toward light.

Monsters unmask when you surrender to me.
Stone breathes and shimmers. Pure delight.

XIX. The Sun

In his mother's womb, the Buddha
blazed; her belly shone
like a translucent shade over a bulb.

Boulders, groundhogs, grass, your surly neighbor—
my light flares from everything.
With all shining, how can you not celebrate?

Let me melt
your stubborn sorrow, leave you
innocent and lovely as an animal.

XX. Judgment

When you come to a fork in the road,
take it.
　　　　　—*Yogi Berra*

One path's cushioned with leaves
whose shapes you traced
in childhood with crayon.

Take the other.

I understand
you don't feel ready.

No one ever feels ready
but you are choiceless as a chick
inside a cracking egg.
Can't you feel yourself
unfolding toward the shards of light?

XXI. The World

Once the world disguised itself
as a dark cave, every creature
fenced by skin and fear.

Now
illusions shatter
like dropped cups.

Zero is an egg that holds all numbers.
The eager dog of the heart
leaps in its fur of light.

The Minor Arcana

After enlightenment, the laundry

—Zen saying

Wands

King—Hercules in Retirement

Let the young bucks labor.
Let some new

fool shoot arrows
at the sun. My sword

and shield rust in a trunk,
though I still wear the Lion's

skin and let its head slip down
to make the grandkids shriek.

It takes a different strain
of courage not to drain

each river that reflects
my shrunken shoulders,

not to pulverize the joints that creak
and mock me when I rise.

On my wall, the Hydra's
taxidermied faces smile.

Queen—Lilith's Daughter on a Date

Boiled to angelic iridescence, the trout
on your plate shines.

Fish are souls not bound
by mammal skin,

the burdens of cow or Jew.
Bloodless, they evade

the Law. I am
a wave chained to the moon.

Punish me for its brightness,
but I will not

shave my dangerous
hair. Who's to say that rage

cannot be carried on a chromosome,
the second X,

the extra cross to carry?
I'm no fool—if Pharaoh

let me choose,
I'd grab the jewels,

my un-singed tongue a serpent
poised to slither down your skin.

Above my bed, a golden
calf gleams. Be my chosen one—

marked man
with the scarred mouth,

peeled sex smooth as fruit.
My legs part like the sea.

Knight—Prometheus Examines his Motives

It wasn't only pity,
though they huddled thin-skinned
and shivering, gnawing raw food,
while animals got feathers,
wings, speed, fur.
Nor to show my brother a fool—
He does that well enough
without help.
I had no plan.
The torch stood unguarded
while earth froze; winter's first
flakes began to fall.
My hands reached and grabbed.

Shackled to this rock
whose crevices and mica-flecks
I know better than my own heart,
I search for understanding,
want my reasons revealed the way
my liver shows itself to the probing beak.
Was I noble?
Scapegoat? Savior? Chump?
Who knows why a god
or man does anything. Punishment
brings no insight, just a dull,
pain-induced detachment from the body
which muddles everything further.
Mornings now when the eagle approaches—rapt,
unstoppable—for a second
while he seeks the spot to penetrate,
his absorption feels like love.

Page—Boy on a Hothouse

Your sneakered feet shade
the limp-petalled lilies, ferns
burned brown in their pots.
Crouched on the glass roof,
you hug your knees, hiding
from Father, who enters like an angry
god to grant water
from a cracked green can.

Mottled pansies droop in a row,
purple as your mother's eye, bright
as the knife you grabbed
and pointed at his chest
to make him stop. How long
can you wait here, August
sun branding your neck?
How long until somebody sees?

10. My Brother's Collections

It started with the acorns
littering our lawn.
Capped or bald, nibbled or whole—

he wanted them all.
When the wind picked up and Mom
tried to end the collecting, he exploded.

He was still throwing rocks
when my father got home
and forced him into the house.

Things got worse with action
figures (bookcase overturned). Dragons
(phone torn from the wall).

Mostly he wanted monsters—horror movie models
painstakingly glued and painted, then shelved
away from my young, clumsy hands. Stuffed mummies

and King Kongs he'd sometimes share.
Inflatable Frankensteins Dad turned purple
trying to blow up. Swarms of glow-in-the-dark bats.

My brother heaped creatures
on his bed. Slept scrunched to the wall,
surrounded by plastic eyes and felt claws.

Dad patched kicked-in doors
and told me, *Some boys
have a temper.* Cracks

showed through the new paint.
Mom's fingers trembled on the steering
wheel. She scoured malls

to find the final members
of his latest set. He was a bomb
one missing Dracula could detonate.

9. Rope

In a harness hung from the ceiling, the children
soar above our heads.
My daughter first—it's her birthday.

She squeals, giddy with flight. Returns
to earth red-faced and proud.
Each girl takes a turn while

others yell her name.
As the last girl swings, one rope
snaps.

The harness arcs. By less
than half an inch
she clears the metal pole.

The kids are hustled to a bouncy castle. I stand
shaky in the cluster of mothers.
At night my daughter glows

while she relives her forward flip,
friends' cheers. Gold flowers
for her newly-pierced ears. Seven candles

snuffed in one blow.
I see the broken rope. The girl,
the pole. The inch's fraction

between them, grace
or pure dumb luck
which may not hold.

8. A Bird! A Plane! A Frog!

After the mad scientist is foiled,
his bomb buried so deep in the earth
its explosion hurts no one but Underdog,
my daughter, naïve to movies, sees
the limp beagle and pleads,
He's not dead, Mom, is he?
This is a remake, so Underdog's a real pooch—
no job shining shoes, no secret energy pill,
though this was cut from later seasons
to keep kids with superhero dreams
from gobbling their parents' medications.
TV now shows preschool beauty queens amp up on Pixie Stix;
one mom serves her toddler
a mix of Red Bull and Mountain Dew.
Yesterday Lance Armstrong told Oprah
he doped for every win.
The second-place finishers won't get the Tour de France titles—
they took steroids, too. Is it cheating
to hold the camera so long on the motionless hound
my daughter starts to sob, though every grown-up knows
his eyes will flicker open
for a happy ending and a sequel?
In my favorite episode, Simon
traps them in a tank and lets it fill. Worn out,
Underdog stands around spouting poetry
while sweet Polly Purebred dives
again and again to the bottom of the rising water.
If at first you fail your deed…
Travis Tygart spent years and taxpayer millions
to prove Armstrong lied.
We want our heroes humble and lovable,
though Shoeshine pines hopelessly for Polly. He can't compete
with his own superpowered self.
Speed of lightning, roar of thunder
How our lives
swelled with possibility when he defeated death
and soared over mountains—
eyes bright with dollar signs and American flags.

7. Mother Lion

The tawny, long-necked lady talking
on a rhinestone-studded cell phone
who drove her Cadillac into a cab
which knocked into the back of my car
where my son slept in his plastic seat,

now gestures, graceful as an antelope,
apologizes to the taxi's beefy
passenger while we all
stand in freezing drizzle waiting for the cops.

She ignores me,
a short woman cradling a baby, crooning
The cow jumped over the moon.

She has no idea
had the cab hit harder, forcing
glass and steel through my son's skin,
how easily I would leap
the distance between us and tear out her throat.

6. Another Treatment

The difference between hopelessness and remission,
Dr. Revici claims, can be measured
by small changes in pH.
I buy a package bulging with glass bottles.
This one drink, these two inject.
The others put in capsules. Write down
alkaline or acid. Very simple.

Three times a day I pee on a strip
and wait for color to rise.
You're a swimming pool, my husband jokes.

In childhood it was my job to test the water.
I dunked the plastic rectangle
until both compartments filled, then carefully
carried it to the basement shelf where chemicals
were stored. Shook the bottles. Added three drops
to each side and watched the water bloom.

Too red meant a cup of powder poured
in the deep end; too yellow and I'd unscrew the top
from the chlorine bucket, eyes and nose burning,
grab a tablet and take it to the filter's net.

My brother and I swam for hours, diving
for pennies our parents threw, taking turns
with the good mask. I could hold my breath
the whole length, slide my belly across the smooth
bottom, practice somersaults and handstands
until my fingers pruned and lips blued.

One day I tried laps.
Winded by five, I took weeks
to build to ten. Another week to fifteen,
then twenty—breaststroke, backstroke, crawl—
a steady striving through water
suddenly spacious and yielding as sky.

Thirty-five, thirty-six, the water
chilled in spots weak morning sun had yet to find.
Forty-seven, forty-eight, my rhythm
the earth's rhythm, fatigue fallen away. Sixty,
sixty-one, sixty-two, I swam
beyond thinking. Beyond time.

Ninety-nine. The final push
of feet against side,
glide, then stroke, one hundred.
I pulled myself out,
stood dripping and triumphant on cobblestones;
gulped the sweet late summer air. Certain
my body could do anything.

5. Captions that Twirl

Painted on posterboard above the hand-written story
of his trip, my daughter's stuffed penguin celebrates
Christmas in France. Fuzzy looks fine
next to what most second graders brought
for "Holidays Around the World"—sagging felt
candles, clay camels, a cardboard mosque.

A few read from scripts
in videos edited MTV-slick, with segued
soundtracks and captions that twirl. *Parents
did the work!* my husband fumes. *That's cheating.*

Once I made a few crude cuts
with an Exacto knife, then let my father carve
an intricate Kachina doll, which I painted
and brought in to classmates' oohs and ahs.

When the principal banned sweets
the day before our daughter's party, we stayed up
past midnight trying recipes for whole grain bread.
The other birthday child snuck in
bulging chocolate cupcakes frosted blue.

Home with a bagful of crayoned
flags, my husband hangs Fuzzy's journey
on the wall while the radio blares Wall Street's
latest scandal and a guilty verdict for the former Speaker
of the House. *At least we're teaching her integrity.*
Most kids threw away our heavy
bread. I got an A+ on the Kachina doll.

4. Tether

Capricorn child, earth girl,
you drive me from the water tank to the floor.
Hands and knees—the posture
I hated in birthing class.

Finally your shoulders
force through the ring of fire,
now your downy, blood-streaked back.
The midwife tells me

to reach down and lift you
those final inches
out of my body
into the bright world.

The chord between us
throbs.

                   *

My mother folds diapers.
She and I laugh, finish
each other's sentences.

                   *

Now,
again and again
you compel me

from the photo albums
I sob into, my mother
gone before your skull bones close,

over to the changing
table or bed. Your hungry
gums on my breast.

Your placenta wrapped and frozen,
to be planted
underneath a tree, in spring.

3. "Adam and Eve, Not Adam and Steve"

My born-again aunt-in-law has no idea,
when she buys my daughters Bridal Barbie,
what she's starting—
Their only Ken's not fancy enough
to match, missing a shoe besides;
so they dig out their other white-gowned doll
and all afternoon make the two women marry.

In childhood I spread Barbie's legs
and forced her onto plastic horses—
jockey or ranch hand. Later I hated her
for the scrunched feet and waist/bust ratio
that would topple a flesh and blood woman.
Now she's an ally.

True, my daughters mostly dress and undress
the guests, trade halters and skirts, argue
over the highest heels.
But now and then there's a ceremony,
and, amid giggle fits, a kiss.
Let's take pictures, show Aunt Bea
how much you like her present.

Spitefulness is a sin. I'm saved
by the girls inviting me to play instead.
I dress Skipper, spiky haired
from a beauty school game, in a gold glitter
bra and mermaid tail.
She's wearing that to a wedding?
I add a fuchsia muff.
She's the Merqueen, bringing
treasure for the brides—
shell barrettes, a tiny golf club,
Ken's remaining shoe.

2. Curious George and the Nazis

Hans and Margarete Reyersbach spend their days
watching animals.
On a windy trip to Europe, Margarete knits sweaters
for their pet marmosets.
The monkeys die anyway. Margarete shortens
her name to Margret; they truncate their last name to Rey
and live with two turtles in Paris,
where they write a children's book
about nine homeless monkeys
and a lonely giraffe. Raffy Giraffe
can be a seesaw. Up-down, up-down.
Mother Pamplemoose and her children
are thrilled. They tie strings
on Raffy and play a friendship song.
The monkeys have skis,
but Raffy doesn't see any snow.
Would you be so kind...? She bends her neck
and the monkeys schuss down it.
Now they make her into a sailboat,
afterward pull off her wet skin
and hang it to dry. *It's rather complicated
being a giraffe.* It's rather dangerous being a Jew.
The Reys must escape,
but how? No car, the trains full or not running.
A bicycle! Curious Fifi can ride backward,
do tricks on one wheel.
The bike shop is sold out. Hans buys spare parts
and builds two bikes. They pedal for miles,
hours before the Nazis enter Paris,
then sleep, surrounded by cows,
on a bed of hay. So many refugees,
so many hours
waiting in lines. Mother Pamplemoose's family
is famous—the Reys are allowed to sail to Ellis Island.
Raffy Giraffe is changed to Cecily G.
Fifi is rechristened George.

Ace—Sunset

Don't tell me pollution
makes these numinous

magentas, that a clean sky
never burns so bright.

I'm not listening,
I'm lost in

sun. My lit heart
hovers near the mountain.

Swords

King—First Meeting with the Guru

Up the twisting driveway to his brick house, I examine
my breath, hope my seven-minute headstand
satisfies this famous, hundred-year-old yogi who, they say,
unties samskaras with his gaze.

When I knock, the door's pulled open
by a skinny teenager, one finger
to his lips.

I follow him to a room
whose windows frame a mountain
half eaten by mist.

Rows of students cram near the platform.
The master's face shines,
florid. Tears pour from his eyes as he reaches
into a bowl of chilies, pops
them one by one into his mouth.

Finally a woman in front raises her hand,
at the teacher's nod, asks,
Great One, what's the lesson?

He smiles. *I am looking
for the sweet one.*

Queen—As Though You Owned that Time

Grandma, your paintings shine from frames. Soap
carvings of rabbits, arch-backed cats, a dancing bear,
two dogs with curling-ribbon
collars march on a tray near your collection of miniature spoons.
Weddings to one side, your mantel
teems with offspring who crowd the self-published volume of your poems.
In each crevice of this house, you put yourself, inking
political slogans on wooden stools, crocheting hats to hold a roll
of toilet paper, knitting handles for the drapes.

When anyone would listen,
you recited Shakespeare, your rich voice filling each soliloquy.
I gave you "Howl" in return,
which you hated. You were even more disgusted by my teacher
and his line "the dead put on their shoes."
"The dead put on their shoes?" That isn't poetry.
It makes no sense.

You know now if it makes sense or not.
But which shoes?
The shiny black ones of your girlhood when you took
the train to school,
and, too small to push open the doors, often had to ride an extra stop?
The heels of your brief rebellion?
The flats for your one job, stenographer at the Aetna, where you got fired
for getting married? (Though they
kept you on, you told us proudly, longer than policy.)
Perhaps the flowered slippers
waiting near the couch where you read.

Absence makes you nicer.
We praise your volunteer
work and amazing memory, ignore your narrow-mindedness, your fear
which made my mother's
childhood a list of "don'ts." *Don't swim, you'll get*
wet. Don't ice skate, you'll
get cold. Don't get a dog, they die.

Twice you broke
this last rule and brought your daughters wagging bundles;
both times you changed
your mind again, with a weak excuse gave the puppy back.

There are things I could tell you,
you said, then clamped your mouth shut and tightened
your throat until something grew there.

Instead you told happy tales beginning, *In my day*
as though you owned that time,
smoothing over the Depression, savoring your sixty years with the
same man.

Grandma, ninety-two
is not enough. This is the last time your house will hold you.
Already the great-grandchildren
are taking paintings; my aunt is offering your bedroom set.

Knight—Don Quixote

Only a fool can't tell
the kinship between a windmill
and a giant, can't see that wolves and warriors
must rise up when the moon holds her breath.
No one, Dulcinea wails, *understands*
the fear that curls like a cat on my chest.
Take heart, Maiden—We all share
the dark, all journey toward
the graveyard's toothy grin.
Let me save you when dreams
sputter and sun's
pallid orange lacks conviction.
Onward, Sancho, though the knight's road
winds and narrows, rich with shadows,
leads to a crow-infested oak whose roots
suck tears and answers underground.

Page—It Might Pop

The rainbow-wigged lady
twists balloons into beasts.
Who wants a turtle? Who wants a snake?
She's billed as a "singing clown"
but only chatters, and always
the same shtick—enormous
mouth twisted in mock terror, she squeals,
I'm afraid of lions or *I'm afraid
of giraffes,* handing off the animals
like burning coals.

Children wave wildly
as she calls *Monkey? Frog?*
My son is still.
I don't want a balloon.
It might pop.
This morning the vet called
about his favorite cat.
Doctors can't fix everything,
but we can love and pet her while she's here.
He nodded, then went off to draw.

Bright balloons
swell like tumors.
The other children crash
their animals, making ferocious sounds.
My son ignores the clown's coaxing,
How about a zebra? A baboon? Zealous
in refusal, safe
in the protection of his empty hands.

10. Like or As

Our son is learning similes.
The sun tastes like a lollipop.
He stretches, gnaws his pencil. *How about
'It sounds like crackling flame'?*
Even some stoked fires fail. Last week
you moved into the basement, now smile
only at the children, order take-out
on your nights to cook. Our conversations
smell like eggshells, taste like bark.
Our daughter cuts paper
body parts, ignorant of her disrupted future,
of how love can shrivel
like the clove-pocked apple slice
we hung above the sink. She slips,
decapitates a lung. Outside, dull December
sun tries its best. The coffee I make for you
out of habit grows cold.

9. Festival of Light

Near the table's edge,
my daughter's dreidel wobbles—
a game of chance she can win.

I guide the fire
and tell a fable about miracles.

Last year my mother
lit the menorah, Dad by her side.
She was weak from chemo, and that story
of tenacious flame fed our hope.

Now she's in the hospital, won't let us come.
When I'm home.
Her voice sounds far away.

Her voice sounds far away
when I'm home.
She's still in the hospital; won't let us come.
She's a tenacious flame feeding on hope,
wrecked by chemo. That story.
A lit menorah and Dad by her bedside.

Last year my mother's doctor
told a fable about miracle drugs,
a machine to guide fire.
A game of chance she could win.

My daughter's dreidel wobbles
near the table's edge.

8. Hep C

Bilious lump, the liver
holds a virus like a grudge. Silently

festers for decades.
My doctor offers 40-60 odds, a year

of fever, hair loss, muscle pain,
anemia. Calls me foolish for refusing.

The herbal master mutters,
stagnant anger, hands me

heavy sacks. I boil,
then choke down the odiferous brew.

Acupuncture, soul retrieval, a slick
hypnotist's low drone, powdered

clam shells, oil of oregano, green tea...
Before, I was

a lucky midlife woman planning
family camping trips. Now,

beaten by the long arm
of the body's law,

I am a cautionary tale.
The one that almost got away.

7. Slowly, Dangerous

Thick, gray sky obliterates
the willow, jagged rocks
beside the frozen
lake. In its melted center, miles
from the woods where hunters' gunshots
shattered branches,
geese dive and swim.
Is one safe day possible?
The geese's urgent honking
follows me home, where one long worm
pours itself along the walkway
and smaller ones scrawl patterns nearby. I tread
slowly, dangerous in my hiking boots.

6. Friendly Floatees

The ocean is pocked with plastic—
28,000 ducks, plus some beavers, turtles, and frogs.
Smiling painted bills bob in the waves.
Intended to float in bathtubs,

28,000 ducks, plus some beavers, turtles, and frogs,
were tossed from a cargo ship in a storm.
Intended to float only in bathtubs,
they make it to the Arctic, drift in blocks of ice.

Tossed from cargo ships in storms,
up to 10,000 crates per year spill into the sea.
Some make it to the Arctic and drift in blocks of ice.
A load of sneakers teaches scientists about ocean currents.

Up to 10,000 crates per year spill into the sea
unreported. No headlines, no books.
Teaching scientists about ocean currents,
after 17 years, Floatees reach the Atlantic

and make international headlines, two children's books.
The toy company offers a $100 per duck reward.
Hearing that Floatees have reached the Atlantic,
artist Marga Houtman builds them a giant duck mother.

Though the toy company offers a $100 per duck reward,
fewer than a thousand are captured.
Marga Houtman displays the giant duck mother.
Britain Prepares for an Armada of Ducks.

Fewer than a thousand are captured.
Britain Prepares for an Armada of Ducks.
The ocean is pocked with plastic.
Smiling painted bills bob in the waves.

5. Animal

When I call *Come* and the dog trots over,
I'm amazed. *Sit* and *Stay* work, too,
and my body tingles,
suddenly taller.
I never believed I could influence
the animal nature of the world.

This morning, after a week
of stagnant heat,
my husband woke surly. As we cooked
separate breakfasts in our cramped kitchen,
I accidently bumped his bread
with the almond butter jar. He glared.
I shoved my stuff near the toaster, washed
berries in the bathroom sink.
Childhood's strategy: *React. Adapt.*

Tonight he'll come home softer.
We'll share pasta, have sex.
I'll almost forget
the new knots in my back.

The puppy jumps up, nips me,
wants to play. I make
the growly sound the trainer taught me,
add a clap and stomp
when she persists. After three tries,
she quiets, flops at me feet. My shirt's
torn from her teeth.

4. Eurydice to Orpheus

I have let go; I opened my hands. Free
in this dark land, I drift, memories
unwinding like thread. My belly
blank, desireless. I do not miss your lips.
Foreign and diffused, your lyre notes drift down. Sing
to someone else! I am not your flower; I am pollen
brought to flight with every breeze. You would bind me
in a dying skin. You take my hand and call me
by my secret name. I follow as I must: I am a woman.
My heavy limbs leave tracks in the damp
ground. I tread slowly, doomed to life, my
love, unless you turn around.

3. Divorce Court

I begged Jesus for his faithfulness! The woman
waves *The Power of the Praying Wife.*
The man won't look at her, shifts his feet
while the judge ridicules love poems he wrote
to a girl with *hair like wings of night, eyes
like brown suns,* and his wife explodes,

What about my *eyes?* My *hair?*
She is twenty-four, looks decades older.
Already I see the cracks in my marriage.
I had thought that love and time
would smooth them to character, the way
a homely teen becomes beautiful when touch

and choices help her find her face.
Now I don't know.
I think about the woman whose passionate
poems of married love I always envied,
dumped for someone else before
the last book came to press,

and I hate my husband—
not the man beside me laughing
at the woman's wails, but my future husband, the one
who will leave me or bore me into leaving him.
The world's failed marriages crowd us on the couch.
My husband changes to a cartoon.

2. Rats Live On No Evil Star

Palindromes show us the truth:
a thing turned backward
stays itself.

The weak wife and her domineering husband
with *no word, no bond, row on*
through years of mirrored marriage

while the sober drunk, bullied by memories
of *night, fifth gin,* now leaves his family
to hide at work.

The corporate tyrant barking on all fours
before a bored, black-leathered Mistress yelling, *Go, dog!*
changes nothing,

nor do teens who run away to live free
but end up jailed after committing *murder
for a jar of red rum,* or tied down by the street's invisible rope.

Starving then bingeing, knowing
reversals make a circle, *we panic in a pew*
but find no answer in the hymns' soft lull.

If I had a hifi, I would play the song of wholeness lost
when Rome's goddess Diana made time start
by throwing rodents into heaven to make stars.

Ace—The Story

Rivers trickle to dry beds.
Sun sucks the remaining moisture
from crumbling banks where children don't play.
For all human time, the mountain has stood.
Its peak slices the labile sky.

The endless tale of endings and endurance
whispers beneath us
as hearts and bones become earth.
Pushed onto this dust,
the newborns wail.

Cups

King—Love Song for Lou Reed

Dead, you're the critics' darling. When I was a teen, you were mine.
Each morning I lifted The Velvet Underground and Nico from
its sleeve, watched it spin, waited for Sunday Morning's opening
notes to warm me like a junk rush. Bursting with things to say but
needing someone else's words, I wore your face to class, read
Delmore Schwarz because you praised him. Your stark songs closer
to Keats: *Beauty is truth, truth beauty.* We both grew up, shed skins.
Left New York City. Learned Tai Chi. I still blared your records,
cheered at my daughter's concert when the third graders sang I'm
Set Free. Now the slap of finding out your borrowed liver failed.
Brian Eno said your first disc sold just 30,000 copies but every
person who bought one started a band. He was wrong. It sold more
than that. And some of us became poets.

Queen—Vivienne Eliot

Really, Tom, it was a toy knife,
harmless as a pen.

Am I mad
to love you so?

Tossed in the air,
lilacs hovered. Sun gilded the river

as our knees touched in the punt.
Captain, I will never tell

about your powdered face
and secret flat, the pretty

dancing boys. A woman's body
smells and bleeds.

I scrubbed the sheets and shopped
for silk shirts, velvet dresses.

You sent me to the country,
then to doctors, doctors, doctors

whose pills nibble me like rats. Do you ever
say my name? I possess you

only on the radio, your cryptic love
poems crackling with static.

Tom, behind these locks
I wait and rot. I bake

chocolate cake, your favorite,
each week, just in case.

Amazon—Persephone After

True, the first time I went willingly. What girl
could resist his leather pants

and rock star swagger, switchblade
in his pocket, my name

quivering between his lips? How better
to escape Mom's pretty vines

than to sway in a poured-on miniskirt
across hell's endless

dance floor while stretched skin
drums throbbed? My gut burned from pomegranate

juice and vodka. The goth house band keened.
Match light flickered on his skull ring

as he whispered smoky promises and blackened
bottoms of bent spoons. His touch

wiped out every ache or question.
My straight-A vocabulary whittled down to *more*.

Soon my dependence
angered him. He gestured

at my puffy eyes and flat hair.
Turned away with a slap.

Mother hauled me home.
A month in rehab, then a shopping spree

for high-necked shirts and
frilly dresses. Good-girl life

to slip back into like the cloak
I dropped on my way down.

Triggered by a song,
a whiff of sulfur—

in any season, broken
ground inside me opens. Memory

drags me back.
Put off by my pink

cheeks and filled-out limbs, the shades
won't know me now.

I try to tell my mother what I saw there.
How I lived. *All that's over. Let it go.*

My friends steer the conversation
back to fashion.

Page—Magic

My daughter's mesmerized by Hogwarts—
Harry's struggles more compelling
than my tries at conversation,
or even calls to meals.
The third grade's preparing
for testing. Homework dittos
multiply; yesterday they practiced
blacking ovals with sharp No. 2's.
Who wouldn't rather turn time back
and soar to freedom on a rescued hippogriff?
Much of her life (I hope)
is still play and ease—food cooked
and clothes cleaned
as though by elves; the magic
of fall leaves we iron onto wax.
Still, every human heart
craves escape, longs to let go
into sugar, sex, wine,
words that carry us across
four thousand pages of a land
where broken things mend
with a wand-flick, and venom's
remedied by phoenix tears.
Responsibility and pain
forgotten. Our ordinary,
mortal bodies left behind.

10. Tenth Anniversary

To celebrate, we watch ourselves—
bright, slim-waisted. Matching in white.
Your jaunty bow tie, my crown of flowers.

The circle's cast.
Our daughters hum
inside my ovaries and my young mother
beams as we kindle one pillar
with two wicks. Now, as then,
my breath catches
at the priestess's billowy sleeve,
the sliver of air between satin and flame.

We make two sets of promises. The first
we've written: Your pledge to guard
my art. My earnest Spanish.
The traditional vows I've memorized
and speak one line at a time:
By seed and root, by bud and stem...
You echo, our voices weaving,
high and low tones in contrast, the way
your dark skin shines against my paleness
when we make love.

Nestled together, legs entwined,
we're wise now, understand
the deal we struck. My sloppy housekeeping,
your temper. My stubbornness,
your loud TV. The push apart, the turn
to stagger back—marriage's excruciating
dance, our small house crowded with a whole
menagerie of *better*s and *worse*s. Their silky pelts, soft
ears. Their wings and wild cries!
Also, snarls in the middle of breakfast, crap
on the floor, fur flying as arguments
chase their tails. Love
crouched just out of reach.

The pair onscreen
have no idea.
Rings are exchanged, the broom
placed on the ground.
Hands bound together by silk cord,
we jump.

9. Many Parties

Guess which vegetable I am,
crows a woman in a caftan, leaning
on the mantle. Two guys play catch
with someone's bra.
This is how we waste our weekends.
Put on eyelashes and make dip.
Twirling light prints everything
with pink and purple stars.

At my family's during holidays
everyone gorges while exchanging diet tips.
There is danger in the turkey, guilt in the pie.
Reagan and Kennedy make
their entrance with the stuffing; religion
keeps us going through dessert.
Then we are saved by basketball or Vanna White.

At poetry parties we kiss lipstick on the air,
turn our necks as in aerobics class
to see if *anybody*'s there.
We don't drop names, we aim and throw them out.
I put ice on a bruise from an NEA grant,
then fling Helen Vendler at a group of formalists.

I'd rather stay home and water the plants,
said a friend whose new baby gives him this right.
I am stuck with people who yell
No, asshole—tomato,
Cheez Wiz aint' a vegetable,
and *Isn't there a vegetable in beer?*

Parties are better afterward
announces a curled up body to no one
in particular. Life is more elastic
in the past tense, can be twisted in the telling
until it resembles fun.
I walk toward the coat pile, trip
on a girl on acid gone on M&M's who whispers,
Wow, incredible. Why isn't anyone writing this down?

84

8. Better than Sex

Now that I don't want them
men flock to me.
There is a mechanic who does my mending,
a wrestler who writes poetry about my biceps,
a poet who massages mink
into my jacket,
a Hindu boy who brings me bits of gold.

Although I warn them
they take me out,
foolishly are jealous of each other,
and wonder why they don't score.

I have stopped sleeping with men,
for the same reason I quit
sugar, which gives a great rush
but saps my energy in the long run.

I need time
to live with myself,
to learn about the treasure
that my skin surrounds.
I cannot share this body
until I claim it.

7. Foolish Teenage Heart,

Desire's pawn,
I miss your brave and wild beat,
your thudding *yes.*
Those dream-drunk years
I didn't know compromise
but knew how to dance
on roof decks under moonlight
when a band or boy or bird
with luminescent feathers
made you leap and I
had no choice but to follow.

6. Missing

Marianne, has it been twenty years?
Or twenty-five?

A plane ticket, a blue silk
dress. A posh café

near ruins. Bloated Roman moon.
Tongue-tied, I wavered.

Longing doesn't fade,
it burrows.

Today your song wails from the radio.
Slaps everything awake.

I dig up a blank card, write,
It's always fall. Relentless sunlight's

cold. Cross that out, start over—
Dull with bills and laundry, most days

I forget I'm hungry. Even forget
I have a soul.

No. *Memory's turned you*
mythic. The only one

to find the lake and show how wind
makes one rock's ripples infinite.

True, but wrong. Oh Marianne,
however long it's been,

I still can't find the words.

5. Memorial Park

Autumn's out of steam. The leaves
on their way to orange
froze in unexpected flurries,
drop without blazing.
Like these trees, I should let go,
but my thick heart's
stubborn as mud. Sucking on fantasies,
I crouch by the lake and fling crusts to ducks,
then rise and turn from the belligerent
quacking, toward a cracked bench
near a log with a sign
designating it a balance beam. Farther back,
a child, grubby-kneed and pigtailed,
tosses a ball toward the sun
and laughs whether she catches it or not.

4. Forty-Seven

Pants tight as a coat of paint,
laughing teens ooze beauty.
They share fruit and kisses at the fountain
where a lone stone gargoyle stands.

I pass them, then stroll by a dark
bar. Some young, ardent rock band
blares. I head home to the bills, my clean sink.
The tiny thrill of items ticked off lists.

3. Independence Day

Though we have a blanket
and an unobstructed view, my older girl
runs with her friends to the wall
at the edge of the field, dangles
her legs into an eight-foot drop.
I stay put until her sister follows.

The younger one in my lap, I sit,
hopefully unobtrusive, behind the clique.
Newly released from second grade, summer-drunk,
the girls giggle and shriek. Some snap
pictures with their parents' cell phones.

I scoot back to give my daughter
space; to my surprise,
she follows. Tentative as a teen boy
at the movies, I creep an arm
around her, wait for muscle tension
or a snippy *Mom!* Yesterday
she yelled, *I hate these jeans, I hate
my life, and everything is your fault.*

Soon she'll disappear
into music and boys, but right now
she leans against me.
Though we're nearing the finale,
the bright bursts overlapping,
and though Rainbow Glasses split the light
into its full spectrum of dazzle, I drop

my gaze to the brown backs
of their heads, then close
my eyes and savor their bodies'
warmth. The hound someone brought
starts to bark, is answered
by howls from over the hill.

2. Why, Because

After our hearts slow down
and our bodies pull themselves back,
with a carelessness reserved
for the healthy, touch me
everywhere again, because winter is stripping
last stubborn leaves from the trees,
and my mouth tastes of ice.

Why the body
so easily vanquished from inside?
Why the soul striving
to live somewhere more durable than this?
Why, always, the mind chopping wood?

Kissed smug and dumb, I want
to squander this morning,
want to lie with you
while my neighbor sings along
as Janis Joplin screeches secrets
through the wall,
louder than the sounds of winter.

Ace—Finally

Love you.

I love you
but when I do,

the isolated *I*
dissolves.

Then there
is only you

and love.

Pentacles

King—Steve Jobs

People who fit in
won't break out

An orchard grows
  in my mind   the cool fruit
        radiant

God's laughter
     I capture
          in a microchip   the future
cries out like a woman
       Take me now

No limit but the body
        faulty programming
        rogue cells' relentless division

Failure is a cliff
If you fall off
          fly

Queen—Lilith to Adam

I have your letters—
Missing you. Come back
to Paradise. Lie beneath me
and the sun will turn us both to gold.

Thank you for the poems, the baskets
of blossoms and fruit.
The threats you do not
sign, carved into bark.

I am not afraid.
When your Father's minions
try to drown me,
Mother's liquid arms raise me to air.

You are the one who trembles
each time feathered wings slice darkness
or a black mare gallops
near the window of your small son's room.

There was no rib.
Our cleaving caused the ache in your side,
a wound that festers
every hour of my banishment; and in

your honest dreams I ride
you while our cries blend
with the screeching wind.

Amazon—The Workshop Leader Tells Us to "Become" a Power Animal

Of course I pick a panther—
noble, glossy, claws sharp
for the face of anyone
who hunts my skin.

Changed to eagle, dolphin, python,
fox, the others advance
making wild sounds. I slink
amid the yapping and flapping,

thinking of Nastassja Kinski.
In the film I watched last night
after my boyfriend called me
too aggressive and *emotional*

and left, Kinski had a sexual problem:
After orgasm
she became a panther
and devoured the man.

Then she fell in love.
Her darling chained her to the bed—
the first safe sex. He got off on
how her come cries turned to snarls.

Tired of padding around this dirty floor,
one beast in a cacophonous
menagerie, I realize
I prefer personhood.

Let a man be the panther.
Let my boyfriend
wake in manacles,
shipped to the zoo

without a good-bye kiss. I'd visit
often at first, but later
might find it hard
to explain to my husband.

Page—Strawberry Shortcake

The young girl turns the rope.
Strawberry shortcake, cream on top.
Her worn Keds slap cement.
Braids flap to the song's beat.

Older boys play ball near the gate.
Strawberry shortcake, cream on top.
Tell me the name of my sweetheart.
It's getting late. The air darkens.

*A,B,C...*Braids flap to the song's beat.
The boys laugh, slap hands.
She calls out letters 'til her foot snags.
Who will be her sweetheart?

Not her daddy, who left. No calls, no letters.
She still watches for him. Waits.
Her foot snags and she stumbles, starts over.
Worn Keds slap cement

as she turns the rope.
She stumbles, starts over.
It's getting late. The air darkens.
The boys watch her, wait.

10. Thanksgiving

For the family crammed around the table.
For grudges parked and locked outside.
For napkins patterned with gourds
wearing pilgrim hats. For pea soup
sharp with thyme. For cars
accordioned on the highway, crushing,
this time, no one we know.
For the birds—the dead one glazed
and sliced, and Agnes,
an Adopt-a-Turkey the vegetarians sponsored,
whose long-beaked face stares
from a photo propped against the wine.
For the wine.
For the children, giggling or squabbling
or sculpting mashed potato caves; one boy
blowing soda out his nose. For the stuffing
of harsh words back down the throat.
For the dog howling behind the gate
who escapes and gulps fallen food.
For the homeless and the poor,
who, we tell ourselves,
are being fed by charities today.
For the President's dumb policies
and the quarterback's fumble, which distract us
from our own faults.
For years thickening like moss
around my mother's empty chair.
For the children.
For the wife slapping her diabetic husband's hand
away from the cake.
For the limited, flawed, earnest ways
we love each other, let us all give thanks.

9. My Mother Graduates from "Model Mugging"

My mother struggles and watching,
      I merge with her.
It is now my foot delivering the kick;
      my knee
      jams his padded groin.
I am back in childhood, the same person
as my mother, one woman
      with two names.

When she breaks his hold,
      I return
      to my body and stare at this strange,
confident woman. She does not need me
to save her.
      How do we
      love each other now?

He lunges, pins her to the mat,
and she becomes my mother again.
      I start to run to her
but am held back by the part of me
wanting my own skin.

He releases her hands for a moment
      but she lies still.
Get up! I want to scream. *You never would defend yourself
so you could never fight for me.*

Suddenly she is everywhere—fists, knees,
legs whirl and land.
      The masked man
      lies motionless.
She stands up and gives a victory yell.

8. Brandeis Senior Year

Things sure have changed since Abbie Hoffman started
Sandwhichman and dosed the tuna fish.
Entire dorms of virgins drink beer, watch Sesame Street, and giggle

about sex. Every week the RA yells
at me and Jenni 'cause we dyed
the sinks. I sell Tylenol to girls in purple warm-up suits,

girls who have crushes on Joey, think his makeup is cute,
and ignore the obvious. Despite regular exterminations
the silverfish return in time for finals. I sketch

them. Pastels scrape paper, lose
pieces of themselves until the air
grows gray and difficult. Stacked in the corner,

my textbooks wait for their
numbers to give them the strength
to fall over.

We feed and shelter subterraneans,
out of pity and for Trivial
Pursuit partners. Only

Eileen can do geography.
When John the Cabby can't answer,
he stalls by pointing out

that my blue graduation
robe is the same shade
as someone's face when they o.d.

7. Galatea to Pygmalion

Perky marble breasts, stone skin, lips
carved in an eternal *yes*—free from all the female

faults you scorn, I shine.
Why do you sing as you dress me in velvet,

string my neck with blossoms and bone? Don't you see
you are alone? Although my beauty will not fade,

I am a broken rock.
The heart you chiseled is still.

Finally you get it—you are mooning
for an inert thing. Inconsolable, you beg Venus

so sweetly that her fire leaps. Silly boy!
Though tears may fool a goddess, I know

my dumb devotion drives you wild.
Your love will die when I live.

6. First Pomegranate

Which part of this crimson
honeycomb to eat? And how? Sun
highlights the knife's blade, stripes the room
like prison bars.

I watch you scoop seeds, then copy;
savor sweet-tart bursts
as red pearls open.
Your food soothes me, your kind,
scratched-by-smoke-and-whiskey voice.
You must meditate, Sweet Pea.
Learn to let go. You're just like me
at that age—beautiful and charming,
far too stubborn.

Not with you.
I read the Trungpa books
you lend me, obey
traffic signs, take vitamins.

Juice stains your lips.
Suddenly clumsy, I spill
water, lose my spoon in the shag
rug. I've had offers, always thought
I didn't fancy women.
        Your blond hair.
                        Your breasts.
No one is that heterosexual.

Now I understand why my ex-boyfriend
sucked a chain of bruises down my neck
the first time I said yes.
Not passion, possession.
"Friend" is a pallid word.
Mentor, motherish though not kin,
I have no way
to mark you mine.

This jaundiced light's
too bright. It slices
my hand as I dig in the devoured
pomegranate's rind for hidden seeds.
Your husband
due back soon.
        Your voice, your hair.
                My hunger.

5. Blues Café

The man at the next table stabs his salad.
A pierced tomato splatters the rumpled
busgirl slouched nearby, who reeks
of cigarettes and sex, probably
from hot nights with a cover band's drummer.
He'll break her heart, the way a boy crushed
mine in Boston, after lust and restaurants
had run their course and there was nothing left
but mumbled excuses. An old story, predictable
as winter. It always starts with a quickening
pulse and ends with snow
some fierce blast drives into trees' brittle limbs.

4. Sweets

I love you like an anorexic teenager
loves chocolate. All boundaries and mastered
greed. Hips sharp, she's memorized
the recipes for Devil's Food, Black Forest—
beats butter and eggs, spoons batter
into greased tins. She won't try a bite, her empty
fork aimed at God.

Vulnerable to you, I might become
one of those moon-faced women, wounded
and obvious, spilling out of a loose dress.

Some nights when we hold each other,
my clenched teeth relax. I taste
how it would be to love you
like a glutton guzzles milkshakes, gobbles
slabs of syrup-drizzled cake. Dizzy
with sugar. All those bony
years of discipline undone.

3. Found Art

Swirling a bouquet of colors on the giant
valentine we're making for my father,
I remember a Brussels hotel,
my dream of art school
on the table between us. *Draw me,*
my father commanded. *If it looks like a photograph,
you can go.* That sketch is long-lost,
though the moment's framed

forever—his face hard in half shadow,
my teenage fingers clenched
on the pencil. The nauseated, frantic erasing.
At Pratt, abstraction and expression were
the rage. My tight, protective renderings
impressed no one. Mr. Klinsing
used my work as an example
of what not to do. *Illustration's down
the hall. Paint like you mean it.*

I mean it now.
Mom four years dead,
Dad spending love's holiday
with us. Forgiveness is an art,
like cleaning a sick wife's tubes. Like living
in the same house after. Her voice
still on the answering machine, my father
tying Q-tips to a ruler
to put ointment on his own back.

My younger daughter bumps my arm,
and aqua splatters the card.
She ruined it! the older one wails.
No, my husband explains, *Mistakes
can be part of the art.* I wet
a clean brush, show her
how to change the blobs
and smudges into a blue
family dancing under stars.

2. Unemployed

No alarm clock. I wake
at the end of dreams, dress for no one,
leave the nagging stack

of bills and saunter past seductive
mannequins and restaurants
to the park. Break a walnut shell;

squirrels take it
from my hand. In Chinatown,
where heaping crates of fruits

and vegetables block sidewalks
next to buckets
redolent of the sea, I deepen

my breath amid honking horns, pause
inside the stillness
between beats so often

lost in the workday's
scramble and blare.
Hanging on silk cords,

carved dragons promise
luck. Metal balls rotated in my palm
chime one high note, one low.

Ace—Fa La La

I want to celebrate Christmas,
my daughter announces. *I want*
blow-up things on the lawn.
She's wonderstruck by our neighbor's
inflatable Mickey Mouse elves.
Behind them, sunglass-wearing Santa, Frosty,
and Rudolph sway, arms around each other's shoulders.
Rudolph must have a leak; his snout's starting to pucker.
Daddy's family's Christian, so why can't we?
Across the street, plastic
snowflakes swirl in a giant sphere.
I try to set aside my filters—
tacky, money-driven, landfill-clogging kitsch—
to borrow my daughter's eyes and see, what?
Spectacle and pageant? Extravagant, in-your-face
celebration? No use. More than the forty years
between us, it's her nature I can't enter—
miles from my anxiety and distraction,
my husband's prickly Brooklyn edge.
No matter how many prayers I chant
or herbs I burn to Brigid,
how many full moon nights I step
onto the porch to wash my skin in silver,
she's the better Pagan—thirty-seven pounds
of joy receptors, songwriter of "Super Day"
and "I Love Everything."
Another neighbor's timer turns on,
makes bulbed reindeer graze. She grabs
my hand, tugs hard. Though it's cold
and dinner will be late,
I let her pull me toward the light.

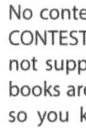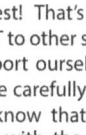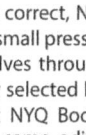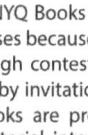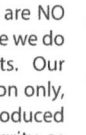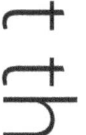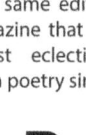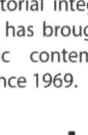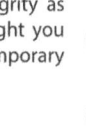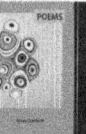

www.ingramcontent.com/pod-product-compliance
Lightning Source LLC
LaVergne TN
LVHW091226080426
835509LV00009B/1182